THE SUN OF HEREAFTER

• EBB OF THE SENSES

Ana Blandiana was born in 1942 in Timişoara, Romania. She has published 16 books of poetry, two short story collections, nine books of essays and one novel. Her work has been translated into 25 languages published in 72 books of poetry and prose to date. In Britain a number of her earlier poems were published in *The Hour of Sand: Selected Poems 1969-1989* (Anvil Press Poetry, 1989), with a later selection in versions by Seamus Heaney in John Fairleigh's contemporary Romanian anthology *When the Tunnels Meet* (Bloodaxe Books, 1996). She was co-founder and President of the Civic Alliance from 1990, an independent non-political organisation that fought for freedom and democratic change. She also re-founded and became President of the Romanian PEN Club, and in 1993, under the aegis of the European Community, she created the Memorial for the Victims of Communism. In recognition of her contribution to European culture and her valiant fight for human rights, Blandiana was awarded the highest distinction of the French Republic, the *Légion d'Honneur* (2009). She has won numerous international literary awards. Her most recent collection *My Native Land A4* was published in Romania in 2010, and was first published in English by Bloodaxe Books in 2014 (translated by Paul Scott Derrick and Viorica Patea), and followed by *The Sun of Hereafter • Ebb of the Senses* (also translated by Paul Scott Derrick and Viorica Patea), an edition combining her two previous collections (published in Romania in 2000 and 2004), which is a Poetry Book Society Recommended Translation.

ANA BLANDIANA

THE SUN
OF HEREAFTER
• EBB OF THE SENSES

TRANSLATED BY

PAUL SCOTT DERRICK
& VIORICA PATEA

BLOODAXE BOOKS

Poems copyright © Ana Blandiana 2000, 2004, 2017
Translations © Paul Scott Derrick & Viorica Patea 2017

ISBN: 978 1 78037 384 3

First published 2017 by
Bloodaxe Books Ltd,
Eastburn,
South Park,
Hexham,
Northumberland NE46 1BS.

www.bloodaxebooks.com
For further information about Bloodaxe titles
please visit our website or write to
the above address for a catalogue.

Supported by
ARTS COUNCIL
ENGLAND

The publication of this book was supported by a grant
from the Romanian Cultural Institute, Bucharest.

INSTITUTUL
CULTURAL
R O M Â N

Cover design: Neil Astley & Pamela Robertson-Pearce.

Printed in Great Britain by Bell & Bain Limited, Glasgow, Scotland, on
acid-free paper sourced from mills with FSC chain of custody certification.

CONTENTS

A Changing Voice for Changing Times

Fragile yet strong, a courageous opponent of Ceaușescu's regime, and an indefatigable civic activist, Ana Blandiana (*b.* 1942) is a living legend of Romanian letters, comparable to the Russian Anna Akhmatova or the Czech Václav Havel. In Romania's dubious post-revolutionary days she was recognised as a symbol of hope and a paragon of human dignity. An aura surrounds Blandiana's name: 'the most noble name in Romanian letters,' as one critic has it.[1] Those who have come to know her are stunned by her charisma, optimism and altruism. Those who have listened to her poetry readings – in the 1980s she attracted huge audiences – have experienced a mystic moment in which, despite language barriers, poetry is communicated before it is understood. In recognition of her contribution to European culture and her valiant fight for human rights, Blandiana was awarded the Légion d'Honneur in 2009 and the US State Department distinguished her with the Romanian Women of Courage Award in 2014. For her book of poems *My Native Land A4* (2010), published in our English translation by Bloodaxe in 2014, she was awarded the European Poet of Freedom Prize for 2016 in Gdańsk, the Polish city of freedom and birthplace of Solidarność. Translated into five languages so far (English, Spanish, Italian, Polish and Catalan), it has been recognised as one of the great European books on liberty.

The poems in this volume belong to two books. *The Sun of Hereafter* (2000) and *Ebb of the Senses* (2004) were composed after the fall of the Iron Curtain while Blandiana was actively and selflessly involved in the public sphere as President of the Civic Alliance (1990-2001), a non-political organisation that made possible Romania's integration into the European Union. These two books mark a turning point in

---

1. Vasile Dan, 'Un nume al poeziei române', *Vatra*, XLV, 1-2, pp. 526-27, January-February, 2015, pp.68-69. All further references to this journal refer to this issue.

Blandiana's poetic evolution: they lead towards a new conception of poetry as a reflection on being that culminates in *My Native Land A4* (2010), whose title refers to the European paper size, A4.

After 1989, the motifs of her poetry remain the same but they acquire a more universal dimension. For Blandiana, the writer is less a creator than a witness of the world he inhabits. She believes that poetry records the experience of one's time and insists that it is 'not a series of events, but a sequence of visions'.[2]

Blandiana agrees with T.S. Eliot that poetry is an expression of both the emotions and the intellect.[3] Her poetry oscillates between the sensual perception of the world and a nostalgia for transcendence. Enigmatic definitions alternate with a series of coded questions charged with melancholic gravity. In fact, her poetry could be seen as a quest for definitions which are reached through a series of questions. Her poems describe the degradation of humanistic values and the different ways in which the individual is being threatened. They express a yearning for a state of primordial purity and an awareness of destructive forces which the self must confront.[4]

Blandiana's meditative lyricism fascinates with its metaphoric directness, aphoristic concision, and desire to express the inexpressible. Her conviction that existence is rooted in mystery turns many of her poems into riddles:

> Poetry is born out of the desire to express what cannot be expressed, out of the obstinacy to define what everybody knows is indefinable, out of the need to offer something which people do not even understand that they are in need of, out of a disquietude so difficult to bear that it becomes an affliction and whose intensity can only be compared with the happiness […] one attains from time to time.[5]

---

2. Blandiana, 'Poetry between Silence and Sin', *My Native Land A4*, p. 100.

3. Al Cistelecan, 'Blandiana "In quarto"', *Vatra*, pp. 61-63.

4. Iulian Boldea, 'Argument', *Vatra*, pp. 44-45; Ion Pop, 'Poezia în căutare de definiţii', *Vatra*, 55-59.

5. Ana Blandiana, *Spaima de literatură*, Bucureşti: Humanitas, 2004, p. 237.

The Sun of Hereafter and *Ebb of the Senses* decry the numbness of contemporary consciousness, the void at the centre of a culture that embraces materialistic consumerism, and the increasing mechanisation and commodification of contemporary life. Her poems, rich in symbols and metaphors, document a turbulent and traumatising period but cultivate a philosophical idiom that fuses the public with the intimate. They adopt a confessional tone that, filtered by Eliot's aesthetic of impersonality, avoids the anecdotal and documentary details typical of the highly autobiographical style of the 1980s.

* * *

Blandiana's involvement in public life during the decade following the fall of Communism left a bitter aftertaste that is evident in these poems. Perfectly aware of the ironic belatedness of her political and poetic work following the fall of Communism, she writes:

> Our century is the century gone by;
> We've become our own history.
> Strange, this sensation of a destiny concluded
> While we still go on existing!
>
> ('Our Century')

She understood political action as a civic concern for moral reform; hence ethical principles should be the core of political life understood as a concern for the wellbeing of the polis. As she loved to remark, the words 'politics' and 'civility' share the same etymological root, the Greek *polis* and the Latin *civita* meaning the same, i.e., city. She placed her moral-civic commitment and her faith that life needs truth, freedom and justice before her literary career. As she later confessed, her participation in the social arena left her with a sense of futility, given the 'great disproportion between illusions and hopes and the time and energy sacrificed in order to achieve a minor change' (*Spaima*, p. 286). During this period she received no salary and her literary production noticeably decreased. She helplessly witnessed the gradual elimination of moral principles from political practice and rhetoric, including by the political group that grew out of the Civic Alliance, a party with the same name, whose representatives exchanged moral integrity for a more profitable opportunism, putting their own interests above the ideals of the Alliance.

Recent history has therefore left its mark on Blandiana's poems. A strong sense of disillusionment grows out of her awareness of a general lack of solidarity with the Other. *The Sun of Hereafter* and *Ebb of the Senses* are meditations on the post-totalitarian phase in which a new, more de-humanised, alienated and alienating order is being shaped. 'Poem' is Blandiana's post-totalitarian response to Yeats's 'The Second Coming' in which no 'terrible Beauty is born'; instead 'Appearances have rotted / And drained away like dirty foam'. 'Newspaper' reflects a country torn apart by enemies who join forces in

> ...a race to the top of the ladder –
> They elbow their way, they share out the spoils
> And they live like worms in a rotting cadaver.
> And so the country continues to breathe
> In spite of this cancer that eats it away.

It comes as no surprise then that the celebrity motif becomes a new theme in Blandiana's meditations. Being a public figure is a wearisome experience that disrupts her lifestyle and leaves her feeling less than authentic (*Spaima*, p. 286). The self is reduced to an abstract, almost foreign name in which 'all that I was / Has been compressed, shrunken / Into the seeds of a few odd letters' ('Starting again'). Very likely, the 'unicorn' destiny that she deplores and others envy in 'Plea' refers to her obstinacy not to let herself be manipulated by others, a struggle she depicts in one of the most remarkable memoirs of our time, *A False Treatise of Manipulation* (2013).

Behind the mask of celebrity, the poetic persona expresses a sense of metaphysical, social and ethical maladjustment. Expelled from primordial time, the self lives in a state of internal exile and yearns for a lost unity that can only be recovered through spiritual love: 'Being entire, being of all. / You and I, undivided light / Re-inventing the god / That is able, alone, to bear life' ('The Whole').

The image of the lyric I devoured by others becomes more and more frequent in these collections. Life seems meaningless and solitude is difficult to bear, while the presence of others is painful: 'It's hard for me to be alone / And harder still to be in a crowd' ('Lament').

Blandiana agrees with Carl Sandburg's definition of the poet as a 'sea animal living on land, wanting to fly in the air.' Poets are the misfits of reality. They strive for an unattainable ideal 'Obstinately waiting for something / That will never happen' and embark on a 'ship of stone' that sails across 'the waves of time' and around which time moves 'faster and faster' ('Ship of Poets'). Blandiana embraces her own maladjustment like a stigma. Poetic creation requires renunciation of the pleasantries of common life and a sacrificial consecration to writing: 'They say I should be happy / Because I chose to die to be reborn [...] You can't be reborn without dying, / They tell me − / Who have never been reborn / Because they haven't ever died' ('Happy You'). She accepts her fate with a willingness to suffer in consonance with the biblical dictum that 'whosoever will save his life shall lose it: and whosoever will lose his life for my sake shall find it' (Matthew 16: 25).

* * *

Blandiana's work was banned for the second time in 1984, following the appearance of four poems in the journal *Amfiteatru*. Conditioned by the grim realities in communist Romania, she began to adopt a direct, sarcastic and denunciatory style which she carried on in *The Architecture of the Waves* (1990), the last book to be written under dictatorship and the first to escape censorship.

Mordant and surrealistic, her poetic idiom renovates the conventions of social poetry in austere reflections on an increasingly estranged world. She laments the disappearance of the sacred, the tragic rupture of a primordial unity of being and the maladjustment of a self immersed in a mechanical present. Dystopian configurations are born out of the self's dramatic relationship with the socio-historic reality of its time. Both *The Sun of Hereafter* and *Ebb of the Senses* document this sense of spiritual sterility and the rejection of a dysfunctional social mechanism. Although history has become absurd, existence is still charged with meaning. Blandiana's lines assume classic and simple forms; they possess 'the nakedness of antique statuary' [6] while they compulsively strive for order and harmony, the principle on which her inner and outer worlds are grounded.

The Sun of Hereafter and *Ebb of the Senses* announce a new paradigm in Blandiana's work that would be completed in *My Native Land A4*, in which, as Mircea Diaconu aptly remarks, poetic expression becomes an ontology.[7] In previous volumes, the lyric I tried to recover the pristine time of beginnings through three approaches – love, dreams and death – in order to recover the lost unity of being. The poet felt a growing sense of responsibility towards the Other and all forms of life and offered to sacrifice herself so as to prevent the degradation of the world. This conception of the self and poetry, as expressed in *The Architecture of the Waves* (1990), is no longer adequate. Society's civic asthenia and the general lack of solidarity render the ethical agenda pointless. The poetic persona discovers that she is unable to save the world from destruction. The tribute of oneself is futile and cancels out scenarios of initiation. Hence the only solution is to anchor existence in the poetic word since 'whatever isn't written down / Doesn't exist' ('The Calendar'). Thus writing has become the reason for existence. The last phase in Blandiana's poetic trajectory is this identification with poetic creation as the only redemptive and defining act of the self. The function of poetry is not to embellish. It has nothing to do with aesthetic decoration, nor is it a matter of the 'glory and pride' of 'those weavers of words, / Who knit their suits and their careers'. Poems are not outward garments, but compose the essential foundation of life: 'poems

---

6. Alex Ştefănescu, 'Un om care nu datorează nimănui nimic', *Vatra*, pp. 59-61.

7. Mircea A. Diaconu. 'Ana Blandiana înainte şi după dezmembrarea lui Orfeu', *Convorbiri Literare*, 3 (183), March 2011, pp. 35-38.

aren't my clothes, / But my bones – / Painfully extracted / And placed around my flesh like a shell'. They articulate a shield with which 'to survive that way / For long and unhappy / Centuries' ('Unaware').

The Sun of Hereafter evokes a world 'Where history was painful / And beat and beat' ('Alabaster Circle'). The lyrical voice assumes the role of the last and first human being trapped in the interstices of an apocalyptic time: 'I am the first of men to grow old / Beneath the sun of these burning skies' ('I Glide, I Glide'). The poems are written from an ominous perspective in the light of 'the sun of hereafter' that outlasts Christ's Crucifixion. The book refers to a world which has lost its orientation, its 'North'. History brings disillusionment and is 'Proof that mankind / Has not condemned its criminals / To death, / But its saints' in allusion to the biblical story of Barabbas. *Ebb of the Senses* continues this agonic perspective. The agitation of the world is contemplated through the neck of the hourglass 'upside down, / Through which Atlantises / Flow towards the sky' ('Hourglass'). The ebb and flow of the senses reflect this turmoil of matter in its constant passage from one bulb of the hourglass to the other, in which the world is periodically inverted and in which 'Neither good, nor evil' exist. Bearing witness to such constant turmoil is the only way of freeing oneself from the chains of repetitive movement and successive inversions.

Blandiana's poetics is a continuing quest for truth. She conceives existence as a perpetual effort to 'comprehend / The incomprehensible'. In an age in which everything is falsified, the poetic I assumes the moral obligation to utter the truth despite the futility of its attempt. Resisting alone 'unmoved, / In silence / And in vain', like 'a rock in the sea' against 'the ebb and flow of the waves' that beat and mould and round off its edges while 'Wearing you down / Into sandy grains' is a heroic act, even more heroic since the speaker knows it is gratuitous.

In Blandiana's universe 'Nothing Happens by Chance', everything is pushed by fate towards an inevitable decline and paradoxically only death can extricate itself from this tightly pre-determined existence: 'Like a seed in the ground / About which all is known: what plant will bloom, / What fruit it will bear, / But not when it will decide / To die' ('Our Century').

Yet is salvation possible? Is there hope in Blandiana's poems? In this opaque universe, only nature and poetry offer ways to deliverance. The poet 'Searches [for herself] in the flower' ('In the Middle of the Way'). Nature is the only realm that has not been affected by the process of profanation. Its purity and simplicity constitute a nourishing fountain for the soul. Weary with existence, the poetic persona longs to become one with nature, yearns to return to 'the groves of old'. She feels nostalgia for this lost paradise in harmony with the universal rhythms and truths that have not been altered and falsified in time: 'Why not go back to the groves of old, / To the silence only the fruit would break, / Where, for ages and ages untold, / Autumn after autumn has rolled away' ('The Knell of Fruit').

Though banished from the polis, the sacred cannot be expelled from nature. Trees possess the attributes of saintliness 'A tree is a saint / That cannot be humbled / Because humility is a part / Of the notion of saintliness' ('A Saint'). At the centre of nature there is 'a sun with the name of god / Who causes the light and the words' ('Light and Words'). The soul feels happy only when it can escape to the reveries of snow ('If We Were Going to Die') or in the innocence of the cemetery hills 'This sensual mound / Like a breast of the earth / So round and alive / I imagine that graves / Are hidden in its flesh / Tied to each other by long veins / Through which / Flow the village dead' ('Cemetery').

As these poems demonstrate, Blandiana annuls the line that separates life and death. Her metaphors of the beyond are maternal reveries of a happy return to a state of initial harmony and plenitude. Imagination changes the terror of death into a vision of light. According to Blandiana, death does not mean the absolute end but 'another perspective and vantage point from which meanings change and acquire another relief' (*Spaima*, p. 250). Death is an indispensable phase for a new beginning, an *ars moriendi* that obliges one to take cognisance of the flow of time and of the essential things in life. Like Emily Dickinson, Blandiana conceives death as a neo-Platonic revelation of the undisclosed mysteries of Being. The earth amazes the poetic I with its transparencies and confessions, it 'feels the need to reveal to me / These marvellous hidden views / While it watches me voluptuously / Descend' ('Transparence').

A new theme in Blandiana's poetry, also reminiscent of Dickinson, is to blame God for the meaninglessness of existence and the unjust distribution of good and evil in the world. The questions she addresses to him are sometimes sacrilegious, yet he descends to approach those who have forgotten him. In *My Native Land A4* he learns to roller skate so as to be close to the young, like parents who learn how to understand their children. However, life is 'A Game of Wills' decided beforehand by a god who has planned everything in advance and who, by allowing no glimmer of free will, transforms the lyric I into a programmed machine: 'What could I want? / I exist because you've / Said that I be: / Like a game of your will / In which you want me to want' ('A Game of Wills').

In *Ebb of the Senses*, the waves of time with their ebb and flow cover and uncover the secrets of existence. Abandoned in time, temples lose their adornments and decoration and reveal their essence, they become 'the simple / Splendid skeleton of time, so much / Purer than when it lived, hidden in the skin' and acquire a nobility they never possessed in life. Death and the past bring out the essence of things and life acquires a purer form: 'Temple ruins are the loveliest of temples / And dead gods most deserving of devotion' ('Degraded Sonnet').

The need for the sacred translates for Blandiana into man's in-alienable need for spirituality and desire to understand the mystery of existence, the 'mysterious combustion / That signifies everything' ('Mandala'). Several poems, such as 'Mandala' and 'God of Pastors', trace the anthropological evolution of the concept of the divine from archaic cultures to Hellenism and Christianity as the drama of the same dying and reviving god, 'gods both murdered and revived, / Unknown, but brothers that live / In this incommensurable neigh-bourhood' ('In Memoriam').

Blandiana reflects on the fate of these gods and the way they are replaced by others. She affirms the fundamental continuity among them. A special place is held by Apollo, god of poetry and music, who arrives 'drawn by dolphins'. 'Brother of the defeated snake' and 'compassionate force' who in atonement for his victory replaces the snake, only to be replaced in turn by Christ, whom he carries on his 'shoulders' in the form of 'the lamb' ('God of Pastors'). From this perspective, Christ symbolises 'The arduous sleep of the seed beneath the earth' which 'conquers death / By trampling down death' ('Pietà'). He undergoes the same dramatic destiny as all other gods of ancient fertility and vegetation rituals, and prefigures our own destiny. Like him and like them, we 'all go into the sod / Only to be reborn, from seed to god' ('In memoriam'). He embodies the buried seed that contains within itself the principle of life and death, light and darkness: 'a light / That is so hard to define [...] With no beginning or end' ('Seed').

Blandiana conceives of God as 'Source of all things, / Geometrical place in the void / That demands to be filled / To come into being' ('Prayer'), that is, she defines him as the silence out of which poetry is born: 'Path by which you enter / A place where nothing exists / If it hasn't been pronounced'. From this 'Supreme silence', the poet 'put[s] forth answer-plants' and engenders 'Trees of sound / So the autumn winds can shake out meanings' ('Prayer').

In Blandiana's mythology the self 'wander[s] through the body of a god' ('The Wound at the End of the World'). This image brings to mind William Wordsworth's neo-Platonic presuppositions of the human being's birth in 'Intimations of Immortality': 'birth is but a sleep and a forgetting; / The Soul that rises with us, our life's Star, / Hath had elsewhere its setting'. She subscribes to Wordsworth's claim that knowing is a form of remembering when she says, 'after all, to imagine means to remember' (*Spaima*, p. 118). In 'Self-Sufficiency', for example, the self shares in a mystery that transcends time and precedes existence. The speaker's individual existence is described as 'A chain of mystery deferred, living / Still, though different, always flowing on / And paying with interest the same old sins'.

The poet is like the 'an arrow from a bended bow', a 'word' tied to 'its etymology'. Just as Baudelaire addresses the reader whom he apostrophises *'Hypocrite lecteur, – mon semblable, – mon frère!'*, Blandiana summons her future readers to accept her legacy as a tribute 'That I shall bequeath unto you when I'm gone / For you to understand, and wisely invest them, / Unborn reader, waiting, like an unborn son…'.

In 'Song of Myself', Walt Whitman bequeathed himself 'to the dirt to grow from the grass' and invited the reader to look for him under his boot-soles. He reassured the reader: 'Failing to fetch me at first keep encouraged, / Missing me one place search another, / I stop somewhere waiting for you' (#52). Blandiana, too, projects herself into the grass that 'Will nurture / The seed of darkness / Of the blinding universe' ('Let Me'). She is reabsorbed into the realm of death and transformed into the seeds that will make possible a new beginning.

Hope in Blandiana's poetry comes from the poetic word itself understood 'as vision and quest for the world's essence which not only gives a greater meaning to our world, but provides the very Meaning capable of rescuing us from futility.' Sensitivity to poetry is 'a matter of spiritual perfection' while 'poets are those who, in a world violently governed by Ugliness and Evil, raise the torch in the name of Beauty and Goodness, transforming poetry into an aura of love and an almost magical shield against hate. This explains, in fact, the confusion that sometimes arises between great poetry and mysticism. Unfortunately, the poet is not the creator, but a witness of the world through which he passes. If the world had been created by poets it would have looked different.' (*Spaima*, p. 264)

VIORICA PATEA
PAUL SCOTT DERRICK

ACKNOWLEDGEMENTS

The Sun of Hereafter was first published in Romanian as *Soarele de apoi* by Editura Du Style, Bucharest, in 2000, and *Ebb of the Senses* as *Refluxul sensurilor* by Editura Humanitas, Bucharest, in 2004.

Acknowledgements are due to the editors of the following journals, in which some of the translations from this book have previously appeared: *The Cincinnatti Review, The Glasgow Review, Make It New, Modern Poetry in Translation*, and *World Literature Today*.

THE SUN OF HEREAFTER

(2000)

North

The power of the sun
Refutes the balance between night and day,
Unquiet light
Like the absolute good,
Proof that mankind
Has not condemned its criminals
To death,
But its saints.

Ocean

Salt on the skin, in sandals and hair,
And crust of salt on eyelash and lips,
Traces of a suffering unequal
Like the sea
That slides, disgusting, through jellyfish hovering;
The sad remains of beings
That seldom share in
The lonely despair
Of seconds slipping away
Or the bitter and
Salt-tinged taste on the tongue
Of half a century
Now consumed, of age, of the year, of motion.
Beach in August,
Ocean.

Landscape

The light in me
Was made so strong that
I could see myself from afar
I could see
In the light of my light,
Beyond the horizon
A world more beautiful
Than I'd ever imagined,
Multitudes sliding
Softly in all directions,
As if on skates or on a sheen of water,
Singing happily, 'Hurry,
Hurry
While we still have light.'
But I was the light,
Shining to the transparent end of the world
In search of the place
Where I could be alone enough
To put myself out.

Self-Sufficiency

I've never been self-sufficient, I know.
Always in the air, hanging – like a fruit from
Its tree, like an arrow from a bended bow,
Like a word from its etymology.

That sense I had, when I dreamed what I would be
Before I came to earth, altered long ago
Into hope forgotten. Now, it wells up in me,
Changing all order, makes me a witness, grows –

A chain of mystery deferred, living
Still, though different, always flowing on
And paying with interest the same old sins

That I shall bequeath unto you when I'm gone
For you to understand, and wisely invest them,
Unborn reader, waiting, like an unborn son…

Ships

Ships made of cobwebs,
Just enough wind to
Make them glide
Across the yielding waves of the fields,
My shipwrecked head at the shore
Like a star
With rays of thorns.
The bending blades of grass are
Licking it,
Trying to tell my head
How hard it is
To be grass and to be wave.
My head can understand:
In the seas of the grass
My head is a ship with roots
That are dying out.

Clock

The clock isn't able
To choose the time.
It has to tell it just
The way the hours come and go,
Bad hour, good hour
One behind the other,
Without ever knowing what it says
So loud
And so hurriedly:
Good hour, bad hour,
Indifferent hour.
Who asks
When all of time is
Past and future
But never
Present?

To and Fro

Sometimes almost ugly,
Sometimes marvellously lovely.
What could I ask for
From my wardrobe mirror
Erased by habit,
If I don't reach my equilibrium
And all the reference points
In the world are tottering
Strangely, more and more strangely.

The mirror
Doesn't decide
To reflect at times the grass, at times the clouds,
In an indecisive to and fro
Nor the day spinning out on the spindle of the dawn,
Old
And forgetful,
Nor the smell of the chestnut planks
Of a gigantic childhood wardrobe;

Only the to and fro
Between life and death
At home,
Coming and going
In the same place,
Like the sea,
Closer
Farther,
Sometimes ugly, sometimes beautiful.

Plea

Help me to weep; help me to pray
Help me to observe my unicorn's fate
With the plaited star of a horn on my head
Stared at in dreams by silent crowds;

Help me to weep, help me to bear
Those avid faces and unhappy stares,
The disdain of praise encircling me;
Help me to pray and to weep.
Help me to curse and to cry
For the world enclosed in my left eye;

Help me to cry and to accept
The secret world my right eye kept;
Help me to cry and to endure the pain
Of shattered images your lifeless eye proclaims
And the inscrutable paradise you hid,
Crushed in the space between your closed eyelids.

I Glide, I Glide

I am the first of men to grow old
Beneath the sun of these burning skies.
Alone I discover,
With no one here to help me,
The tremendous surprise
Of a body that is mine
But is being left behind,
Like a devastated shore,
While I glide
On, glide on above the waves
Until I see myself no more.

Starting Again

To be born again
From my name
As in a rite of initiation,
After decades in
Which all that I was
Has been compressed, shrunken
Into the seeds of a few odd letters?
And now, once again
Shall I search for another fertile
Mound,
Shall I bury the seeds
And obediently wait
For myself to sprout?

But who still knows
What I was before
To identify me, like a cadaver
Closely stared at with
Something like revulsion?
And if not, what good
To be born again and again,
Always to read and write myself
From these same syllables?

Fulfilment

Am I that being in the mirror
Or only a form filled with deeds
Like a burlap doll? Lord,
You don't know how much I yearned
To grow as quickly as I could,
To be condemned by
Reality,
Expelled from the fairytale,
To lose
My baby teeth,
To be suddenly
Overwhelmed
By the enormous wave
That would carry me away.
And everything has come to pass
As I wished for long ago.
A divine irony
Has decided that
All my dreams come true:
I'm an adult.
I swim through the crowds,
I drown in reality;
My steps are no longer anonymous,
They can't walk on water any more;
Although they struggle
My arms can no longer fly.
And now I don't recognise myself.
I've forgotten who I am.
I'd like to go back.
But to whom?
Everybody hurts me.
I feel this terrible longing
For myself.

Happy You

They say I should be happy
Because I chose to die to be reborn.
What else could you want, they ask me,
But no one waits for an answer.
All of them tell me, Happy You.
(And I repeat it: Happy Me.)
You can't be reborn without dying,
They tell me –
Who have never been reborn
Because they haven't ever died.

Clinging to the Branches

Clinging to the branches,
Some of them almost dry,
Others just ripening,
But all of them with wilted and fibrous
Clothes,
And their wings twisted in the wind.
For a long time now they have given up trying to let go
And fall,
As though they knew
That farther down there are other branches
Where other angels
Are withering away.

Apollo

Return, drawn by dolphins to this strand,
Cradling the cither in your hands,
Lapped by the ever-moving waves that come
To contemplate the god
Of these altars
With statues and masters
And with bones of temples, burnt by the sun.

Come softly. Steal in among the stony dead
Entrapped in museums, and admired without piety,
While the earth's weight barks out symmetries
Of metres forgotten, beneath these marble heads.

O Lord, come witness the poetry impoverished
And poets fallen under history's implacable curse.
Beautiful and naked, come. And should you shiver
With the cold, take on the narrow clothing of this verse.

Two Crosses

You were my cross
Tall and thin,
Able to crucify me
Beam on beam.
I was your cross
Child-like, seen
Reflected in the mirror.
One same motion
For embrace and
Crucifixion,
For the bridegroom
And the bride.
Oh let the time
Flow twice, from
Dusk and from dawn,
For one and for the other,
So we seem the same,
And sombrely cover
Us with flowers –
From which we will look up to the sky
Adorned with two twin crosses:
One of them made of shadow.

The Whole

Neither man nor woman,
Neither old nor young.
Neither stone nor tree,
Neither water nor fire.
Being entire, being of all.
You and I, undivided light
Reinventing the god
That is able, alone, to bear life.

Pietà*

Sleep a little more. Yes, sleep on,
The arduous sleep of the seed beneath the earth
So in springtime the god who conquers death
By trampling down death with death will bloom.

Sleep on, and dream how you will bring back
Those who lie in the tomb, and give them life
With a sudden shock of joy that will shine
In the eyes of aged children from the past.

And when, from eternal winter's keep
You awake to the sun of hereafter,
Arise from the arms of Mary, your mother,
And wake us, too, from our sleep.

---

* Allusion to a chant sung during the Orthodox Easter service: 'Christ is Risen/ from the dead/ Trampling down death by death/ Bestowing life/ Upon those in the Tomb.' [Tr.]

Just Visiting

Old ones who tenderly go to the graveyard
As though it were a formal appointment
With the beyond,
Tired when they think that they still have to
Go back home
And cannot stay there
Forever.

The Wound at the End of the World

I wander through the body of a god and
Do not know if it exists
Or I get lost within the confines
Of a different master,
One I have no idea of,
And that, like the other one,
Believes he is unique
And fears
My obstinate will
To keep on going
And thus discover –
Who knows what? –
The wound at the end of the world
From which are still dripping,
Unknown to one another,
Hypothetical gods.

Alabaster Circle

Alabaster circle
Around the eye that understood,
Rounded sign
And false
On the unmoving surface of the time
Where I am;

Darkened circle
Around the eye that believed,
Oval sign,
Infinite half,
On my body, the shore
Of the earth
Where history was painful
And beat and beat
One wave after the other;

Golden circle
Around the eye that has come back to life,
Supreme sign
And triangle
Of love on the temple,
Where I kneel down
And call to him
Only when eternity occurs.

If We Were Going to Die

If we were going to die in the snow
And the only thing left in sight
In the world were an endless
Expanse of immaculate white,

That white would be a symbol of
Our love that points towards rebirth:
Tomorrow we'd be those lovers
That yesterday were buried in the earth.

Still in love, our hair going grey,
And ever passing, clouds that slowly blow
Away to leave uncovered souls,
Like mountains beneath the anonymous snow.

Ship of Poets

The poets think it's a ship
And they get on board.

Let me get on the ship of poets
That sails through the waves of time
Without ever rocking its mast
And without ever having to move
(Since time moves around it
Faster and faster).

The poets wait and refuse to go to sleep,
Refuse to die,
So as not to miss that final instant
When the ship departs from the shore –

But what is eternity if not
This very ship of stone,
Obstinately waiting for something
That will never happen?

Cemetery

This sensual mound
Like a breast of the earth
So round and alive
I imagine that graves
Are hidden in its flesh
Tied to each other by long veins
Through which
Flow the village dead;
This mound like a breast
Swollen up with the abundance of death
From which, when I'm thirsty,
They'll bring me to suckle.

The End of the World

How would everything end, if it ended?
Would it be like the burst in the air
Of a dandelion's globe, suspended,
That scatters its seed as it disappears?

A world that remains alive
Increases itself as it dissipates.
The end of the world, put off, implies
That other worlds will have to wait.

The past comes back in the present.
The future takes its place,
A dead king followed by his lesser regent.
Everything, after it has loved, will vanish,
Flowing all away – no sound, no judgement –
Beneath the sign of the double fish.

Let Me

Let me undo
That terrible seed,
The error of custom,
From the flesh of the happy fruit:
Humiliated, let me hold my tongue
Concerning those things we don't understand
Since we know them by rote;
Let me die
So you can ask: Was she
So close
That we couldn't see her?
My shadow
Dragged through the grass
Will nurture
The seed of darkness
Of the blinding universe.

Ask,
But leave me verse.

No

Not yellow trees, nor red trees,
Nor green trees,
And not the ideas of blackbirds, endlessly repeated,
Just like the stucco repeated
Through numberless rooms
Where no one can be happy;
And not the figs, painfully brought forth,
The sand of their seeds
Behind the fences invented to protect them;
Nor elephants with branches and leaves,
Nor corridors of stamens,
Nothing could be more powerful
Than the magic
Of not having to say NO
Because nothing depended on me.

Ballad

Whom have we murdered
To put in the foundations
Of our house?
If your answer is *no one*
There's nothing to be done but admit
That we've murdered each other
Or that each of us has killed a bit of himself.
A sacrifice was needed.
So that everything can last –
And it's lasting!
But, do we know what we've killed
And how, and what we'd be like unkilling
But alone?

Not One Letter

Not to have a name
Not one letter
Daring
To reach you,
As it doesn't dare
To reach the leaves. Not to speak
(When they ask who you are)
With infinite pride.
And with no explanation
The silence
Suddenly glows
With the light of wholeness.

Nothing Happens by Chance

Nothing happens by chance:
Not the shiver in your spine,
Not the fruit on a branch,
When everything causes me pain –
The honey in the hive
The salt in the sea –
And everything is fated to take the life
Of the child I used to be.

Beneath the Clods of Snow

It will snow so hard that
The birds will fall from the air,
Wings weighed down with enormous flakes
Of a different storm, more honest,
While you lie sleeping there
And the snow keeps falling fast
And no one will know that you're dead
Beneath the clods the swirling snow has made.

A Saint

If you cut off the arm of a tree
Another arm will grow from the knot,
And if you cut off a root
Another root will grow in its place,
And if you tie up the boughs with a cord
They'll still all blossom together,
And if you pick its fruit
There will still be more for you to take.
A tree is a saint
That cannot be humbled
Because humility is a part
Of the notion of saintliness,
A battler
That cannot be defeated
Because defeat contains
The notion of battle,
Just as the seed contains the tree
And the tree contains eternity.

The Knell of Fruit

Why not go back to the groves of old,
To the silence only the fruit would break,
Where, for ages and ages untold,
Autumn after autumn has rolled away;

And the clouds have swallowed up hales
From troubled skies nearby
While, as in so many ancient tales,
Cherry trees murmur cherries in reply.

Yet even in edens the laws
Of legends sometimes change.
But still, in the single tongue they know
Apricot will always be apricot's name.

And, as if nothing in the world
Could mar their hopeful days,
For thousands of years, undisturbed,
Apples are always what apple trees say…

Oh clock of the world that metes
Out seconds with seeds, hours sweet
With pulp and years with alcohol, a century
Drunk with the knell of the fruit in the grove…

There Is No Answer

There is no answer that grows
As much as its question does
Or solves the mystery so well
As the doubt that it compels.

Because there is no light
No matter how bright
Without the dark that one time was
And one day will come back as night.

Definition*

Too beautiful
Not to be conquered,
Too youthful
Not to be mastered,
Too wealthy
To belong to itself.

Too wise
To fight,
Too brave
Not to be wounded,
Too skeptical
Not to be defeated;

Too defeated
Not to be free;
Too free
Not to be humbled,
Too humbled
To die.

---

* This poem is a definition of the Romanian people. [Tr.]

The Middle of the Way

I search for myself
Like the seed that
Searches in the flower
And doesn't
Find itself,
Even though the flower
Is inscribed like a child
On the way
Towards the following seed.
I search for myself
In the middle of the way
In the middle ground
Just as the seed
Searches for itself and goes farther
By means of the flower, in the midst of death.

Confusion

Nothing that surrounds us every day
Is simpler than we are.
Sexes of angels, so far
Banished from these bodies of clay

Are also unable to understand a thing
About the shadow that drips onto the altar –
A confusion in which only fear
Is pure, though probably in vain.

Poem

It's no longer necessary
To destroy appearances:
Appearances have rotted
And drained away like dirty foam
From the face of the essence,
Ugly and eternal.
I can only look at it
If I have enough strength.

Instalments

In praise of breaking, of grinding, of sand
In which you can bury yourself
In thoughts of the stone;
In praise of the wisdom of the crumb,
Ocean of droplets,
Deep, deep crevice;

In praise of the strength to accept the mill
And the humble will of flour between wheat and bread,
Between head and waist,
Between Eleusis and farce:
In praise of you, amazement,
Like a key to
The padlock of reality
That was thrown into the sea.

Nothing entire, not woman, not man, not fragments
Of the single dreamt-of being,
In praise of you, O discontinuity
In praise of you, O particles and elements,
Broken steps, leading
Upward to the ultimate idea,
Everything delivered in instalments…

Hourglass

Neither good, nor evil
Only algae and fish,
Only happier shells
Closed up in themselves,
As a proof that no one loses,
Triumphant sands
Flow among the ruins.

Good and evil
And the sea and time
And verses written
On arid beaches,

When the whole universe
Is an hourglass, upside down,
Through which Atlantises
Flow towards the sky.

Lament

Alone with others,
It's hard, a bitter scent
In the leaves, their recent
Colours fade as they fall
And grinning faces from before the war peek
Out from rancid whitewashed walls.

The worst leave sand in the teeth,
The best brew sour rhymes,
It's hard for me to be alone
And harder still to be in a crowd,
It's hard for me to hold my tongue
And even harder to cry out loud
A truth that is shattered to bits.

But most, I'm afraid, and it's hard for me to try
To drag God back to
The sky.

Buzeşti Square

Oh Lord, let the mongrel and the urchin
Bite into the same piece of bread
Among the heaps of rubble
And the heaps of trash,
Beneath a stultifying sun
That will finally put them to sleep
Curled up, reconciled
With the universe reduced
To that one piece of bread
That still displays the teeth marks
Of the angel.

The Old and the Young

The old and the young,
All so inept,
Some not yet
And others no longer,
While inside the bone where you unmake me
A poor adult is multiplied. Oh, see

What pitiful fragments
With no core,
Those times all equally far from me today!
Tell me where to place myself, oh Lord,
When all other ages are so far away
And vainly,
This child that I still am
Is searching, frightened, for a grey-haired time
Or dreaming
The dream even farther, even wider,
A luminous death, brighter and brighter…

But hopeless, only discovers there
An exhausting eternity that she cannot bear.

EBB OF THE SENSES

(2004)

Mixture

Beautiful necks
    like slippery braided
    snakes,
Rosettes of bodies with skins of stone,
Columns or trunks,
Birds with four, six or eight legs,
Winged beasts with feathers made of metal,
Sophisticated mixtures
    of criteria,
    species,
    conditions,
Confused on purpose and incompatible
In a time that spreads out like a stain of oil
Over the limpid surface of eternity.

Illusion

Inseparable, ineffable,
These two triangles
Pointing up
And pointing down
Enchained, entwined,
Rays of opposite sex
In a single animal
That devours itself with yearning.
Captivating light for a provocative god
That breathes life into realities by saying them
Slowly
One by one:
Woman, man, flower, cloud.
In the twilight of language,
At the centre of the sacred void
Is a god who thinks he is the word.

Old Angels

Old angels, stinking
With a rank smell in their humid feathers,
In their thinning hair,
Their skin peeling off in patches of psoriasis,
Maps of terrifying
Unknown lands,
Furrowed, scored and scratched.
Too sad to bring good news,
Too thin to wield the sword of fire,
They sink half asleep into the earth,
Like seeds being planted
In the rheumatic joints of wings,
Deeper and deeper in the ground,
Older and older, more and more human…

What I Don't Understand

It kills me, everything I don't understand.
The woman who keeps on
Asking for explanations is dead.
She doesn't accept them and goes on insisting,
Since in the beyond
You cannot live without understanding either.
So there you die too, and there you're reborn,
Forever and forever
Only to be able to comprehend
The incomprehensible:
This is a definition of immortality.

To Be a Rock in the Sea

To be a rock in the sea,
In the ebb and flow of the waves
Beating you incessantly
And moulding you,
Rounding off your edges,
Wearing you down
Into sandy grains.
To be a rock in the sea,
An eardrum of infinity
That withstands, unmoved,
In silence
And in vain.

Op. Cit.

Time writes its verses on my body.
They're so complicated
They can hardly be read.
It inscribes its ideas on my skin
Without my permission.
It circles my neck with
Long, sinuous, splendid letters,
Accents my eyes with small print,
And scribbles subtle lines around
My lips.
It thickens them
And then, as at the end of an *Opus*,
It signs its name on my still-round forehead,
Never explaining
Why
It leaves these messages
On me
Or who
Is going to read them
And reply.

A Young Horse

I've never figured out what world I live in.
I rode on a horse as young and as happy as I.
When he galloped I could feel his heartbeat
Against my thighs
And my heart pounded, unquenchable, with the speed.
Everything flashing by, I didn't even notice
That my saddle was resting
On the bones of a horse
That was rapidly falling to pieces on the trail
And that I was still riding
On a young horse made of air
In a century that wasn't my own any more.

Thistles and Gods

Thistles and gods all withered in the sun
Like the blanched remains of temples,
Long and slender skeletons,
Irrevocable examples
Of the burden of being immortal.

As though it were a summer without end
And all of time a single day
Made widow by the night, when
Leaves refuse to fall
And roses, on their pages, stay.

There is no past, no time to come,
Just this one day, endless and spectral.
Above, an immoveable sun
That cannot
Measure out
The senselessness of being immortal.

Selection

Those who have no wings
Bustle round the cloakroom to collect them.
Those who do have wings
Very carefully zip them up.
In the present conditions
It's hard to know
Who will be able to fly
When the moment comes,
When the earth
Opens up
To carry out both a tardy
And useless selection.

Ash

As lovely as a poem
In a language that I don't quite understand,
This time that I am made of
Runs out in seconds and hours and days.
Only a stump
Of the once-tall candle remains
But the flame puts a crown
On the wick, like a goddess's coronation,
Yet,
Crushed by so much splendour,
She lifts it up in desperation,
As though it were a pillar
Of ash, about to tumble down
And scatter, in this ultimate now.

Curriculum Vitae

The sea destroys itself.
It rises up, it crashes into the coast,
It breaks and it turns around,
It beats against itself and falls to pieces.
What does it reproach? What does it shout? Why does it foam?
Shattered in the waves that lunge
So ferociously at one another,
What does it want from this white-green rage
That unravels the horizon
Without even asking
Why it hates itself
Or what it refuses to forgive?

The Line

My God, what a waste!
How I've thrown away the seconds and the minutes,
The hours, the days, the weeks and the years!
The passers-by were fighting each other to catch them on the fly;
They couldn't believe their eyes.
My friends tried to stop me;
My enemies said:
She must have her reasons, something up her sleeve,
No one can be so crazy…
But I was.
I kept on throwing it all away while I smudged
The line between
The sublime and the ridiculous,
Letting them get mixed in together
As bile sometimes gets mixed in with the blood.

A Cathedral of Wool

Spectres with branches,
Trunks with wings,
Wings with leaves,
The fog mixes everything up
Into confusing alloys
Struggling to get free
And fly away,
Trees shed their feathers,
Butterflies row across the mist-held land
And set down tenuous roots.

No kingdoms of flora and fauna here,
No stable states of matter,
No line between the sea and sky,
No shore between land and sea,
And from the depths of the water shoals of fish
Swim up towards the clouds and turn into cranes,
While their cries ring out
Like the ringing of a bell
In a cathedral made of wool.

This Mirror

Between us two
This soft, uncertain mirror
Slanted like this
So that I can't see myself
And you can't see yourself
But I see you
And you see me,
Our eyes meet
And they stare
At this silver horizon.
As long as this mirror exists
And contains us
In its deep deep dream,
The life and the death
In which you exist, in which I exist
Are only tales
In which I exist, in which you exist.

And Yet

How could I stop or give away
This pain by my own light, my will,
More core than ray,
Less luck than guilt

And guilt while I believe after all
In the good that will come into sight
At the top of the highest wall
Built up against the coming night.

And yet, and yet, I defy as before
This time dying out within,
Still undefeated by the evil and the good,

Though feeling more and more absurd
When I find new heavens, again and again,
In the belly at the mortar's core.

Indian Ink

Nothing is so closely paired with
Me as the sea.
I, too, am salt water
Held between different shores
But drawn by the same God.
The moon absorbs me
And the sun goes through me
To be able to rise
Between my eyelids
In the dawn.
The wind stirs me
And turns me into waves
And clouds
So I can fall in the snows
And flow in the springs,
So I can return with
Every wave of Indian ink
That can bear
To rock and to hide
In its deep blue shrouds
The long-dead ships
And the living squid.

Reserve

Horses and poets,
The beauty of a world
Defeated by technology.
Beings that time
Is leaving behind
Imprisoned in
Their own lonely auras.

Horses and poets,
Scarcer and scarcer,
More and more priceless,
More difficult to sell.
Black, dappled, white,
Whiter and whiter still,
Then transparent, invisible,
In a future
Without them,
Invisible in itself.

Eyelids of Water

Eyelids of water
That close, and open and close
Like an echo,
You can hear them before you see them
Coming closer to the shore with
Lashes of foam.
They slowly lean
Above the pupil of stone,
And then they rise again
And all alone
They shut their vision of the land,
Covered with water and sleep
And dreaming a line in the sky
For a moment between the lids of their eyes.

A Game of Wills

What could I ask you for
If, in any case, you know
What I could ask you for?
What could I want
If, in any case, you decide
What could I want?
I exist because you've
Said that I be:
Like a game of your will
In which you want me to want.

Leave me alone for a moment, go to sleep,
Forget me a while
So I can think something
That you haven't already
Had in your head!
Leave me in peace –
A peace that you haven't planned!

Aren't you tired of knowing everything beforehand?
Look, right now I'm making a poem
That you've always known
By heart.

Laurel Leaves

For your sake I chew these bitter laurel leaves
That make
The world spin round
In space and time
And disappear.
Alone, I poison myself
And I change,
I chew and I stutter
Alien verbs, about to give birth
To meanings that flow like dirty foam
From my lips
Without ever knowing
What good it's done me to prophesy
From my own intestines, always
Guilty:
God, god, god,
Light, light,
Nothingness.

Ocean

Ocean as old as an hourglass that
No one has turned for thousands of years,
Only the clouds are able to raise it up
And make it white in the sky,
With mountains of snow on the waves
Given over to dreams and laziness
But nevertheless alive, flowing through the time
That is left, although done, mystery.

Ocean grown old from a tedium
We call simply deathlessness.
Who
Shakes you so in this same place,
Condemns you always to run
From yourself towards yourself
When, staggering from life to life,
The blade of death would be grace.

Oh leave my lifeless body on the shore
Of the end, so that from the beyond I can
Witness your indecision
Eternal cradle, ancient ocean!

In the Absence of Sounds

You, Lord, who permits us to choose
Among so many senses
Through which the world prevents us
From paying attention to ourselves,
You've tried to help me.
In the absence of sounds
The horizon turns thick
Like a soft stone
Through which can be seen
From time to time
A bird that rows
As though it could feel
Its way with its wing
Through the cushioned walls
Of the universe.

Lascivious Landscape

What can be more sensual and more indecent
Than the flesh of the earth
That the sea, at times,
As it pulls itself back,
Laughingly undresses
Like a skirt with dirty white laces
Obscenely lifted from the shore
Where the edge of the stocking
Doesn't quite reach the mystery up higher
And just leaves in sight a narrow band of skin,
Animal horizon
For bad or for good,
Brilliant and slippery depths of the sea
That the sun dives
Into, shamelessly.

The Painted Wardrobe

He holds a scythe in his hand
And he leans politely over
To his beautiful, bashful lover
With a heavily powdered bouffant.

He's wearing wide-bottomed pants
And a feathered, three-cornered hat.
His eyes seduce what they're looking at.
What's more, he's holding a scythe in his hand.

His gesture, replete with extravagance,
Belies its dark significance.
So he shakes his scythe at the void instead
Though he's wearing a woolen wig on his head.

This agèd, macabre Don Juan
Between the dust and the salon
Delivers his risky reply
Exuding a courteous irony.

As everyone knows, in the German tongue,
The word for death is a masculine one.

More and More Alone

More and more alone
With fewer and fewer friends.
So much I was familiar with
Has slipped away
Into the great light.
More and more of them wait for me there
Fewer and fewer are with me here,
More and more alone,
Like a bird
Being forced to migrate
To a warmer land…

Motion

It comes and goes, it comes and goes,
Useless and fleeting, it ebbs and flows,
Momentary thought, foaming and seething,
Smaller and smaller, it breaks on the shore
And then it retreats and returns once more,
The same as a wave, beating like the wing
Of a liquid bird that can sometimes be
Both flowing river and ebbing sea
That comes and goes, in this same place,
Drops brought together at one behest,
Wave after wave, swell after swell,
Syllables of thought, able to kill
But never completely pronounced:
Taken in flight and plunging down to the ground…

Castle in the Water

Castle in the water
The higher it reaches
The deeper it sinks,
Beaten by winds
And moved by waves,
It doesn't exist on the land,
Only in the sky
And in the water,
Much higher
Or much deeper than the real.
Appalling comparison
In which only equality remains unattainable.

Song

Tears and leaves
Sepals and roots,
Fragile tears and round
Tinkling on the stems,
The jewels of a saint
With vegetable forebears
With rings of grass
In their hands like crowns.

Cry the white perfume
That has no source,
Cry for the lustreless
Fate of your being,
And please stay near
When I bolt and run,
Filled equally with fear
Of the old and the young.

A Few Points

Happiness is like
A Pointillist painting:
A few coloured dots
Unrelated,
That sometimes manage to mean
And sometimes don't,
That only manage to transmit
The shuddering of an incomplete
Question
That you don't know how to answer
Because you don't know what's being asked,
You only understand the intensity of the question
Which is missing several points…

Mire

Tears of the victim and
The hangman mixed,
Dirty tears
That wash them both
But do not purify,
They only jolt them to the roots,
The lowest and
Most burning level
Of humanity,
That I try to reach
Slipping dangerously, about to fall,
Losing my balance
In the mire of compassion
And disgust.

Seed

I have pondered it a lot,
And at different ages,
Without any fear, without any pride,
Without any shame
Or bravery or sin.
The sudden approach
Of a light
That is so hard to define
Because it exists alone
With no beginning or end.
And everything is born of it,
Because it only, the eternal,
Is able to preserve the eternal seed
By sowing me,
Scattering me freely
Over the earth.

The Programme

Concerning death:
Some give speeches
Some write poems
And others simply die
Because they can't do anything else.
Around these latter
The rest will come together, pious
And angry because their programme has been spoiled,
As though they didn't know
That they will also spoil the programmes of others
When they can't
Do anything else.

Beach

Foam scattered over the shore like sperm
From the putrefying belly
Of the sea,
And the fallen feathers of birds grown old
And stained with oil,
And the dried-out eggs of long-dead fish,
And thousands of seeds of sand
Inside of which unborn
Unsuspected plants
Have turned to stone.
Everything is barren, uninterrupted,
Only the rays of a burnt-out sun
Continue to wake us up
With the tender power of death.

Transparence

My feet can barely reach
This transparence of the earth.
It overwhelms me with confessions,
Showing me these dead
That are no more than shards of the dead,
Amphoras that are no more
Than broken fragments of amphorae,
Seeds that rot to be able to grow,
Rocks three-quarters buried
That the winds wear down
And cover with the dust
Of their own dissolution.
The earth feels the need to reveal to me
These marvellous hidden views
While it watches me voluptuously
Descend.

Unaware

Obviously, I'm not like
Any of those weavers of words,
Who knit their suits and their careers
Their glory and their pride
Although I mix with them
And they look at my words as if they were sweaters:
'How well-dressed you are!' they say;
'That poem looks so good on you!'
Always unaware
That poems aren't my clothes,
But my bones –
Painfully extracted
And placed around my flesh like a shell,
Following the example of tortoises
That manage to survive that way
For long and unhappy
Centuries.

A Wild Beast

A wild beast.
Who could think
That it's not a wild beast?
Enough to see
The way it lunges between the shores
Like a beast in a cage
That only sees its bars.
Enough to see –
Once the rage has passed –
How the dirty foam flows
Like the spittle of madness
On lips exhausted from so many roars.
Enough to try to caress
Its magnificent liquid skin,
Skin of a beast of the apocalypse,
Impatient,
And, in spite of that, incredibly lovely
For the veritable end of the world…

Swamps

Ancient mirrors, splendour the past bequeathed.
This rusted shining from other days
Entraps you and you breathe in
Exhalations of a cursed fate.

No, not mirrors, but prisons of time
Where you can only see the sinister century,
As you strain to find ghosts
That have drowned and gone away.

You go down deeper and attempt
To reach those sunken shades,
But fear is your only evidence,
While from the metal, ripples emanate

And you sink into these silvery swamps
That close above your head, and lie
                          and lie
                          and lie…

Goodbye

My arms rock the wind
As though their leaves were gone,
Trying to say something
In a language
They don't quite know.
They rock
Unsure, feeling the sense and the air,
Afraid that the trees that stayed behind on the bank
Might misunderstand.

Asleep

When I can't stand it any more
I fall asleep
And, if in my dream
I can still hear a muffled rumour of reality,
I fall asleep in my dream
And, afraid, I listen apprehensively,
And if it reaches me even there,
I fall asleep in my dream within a dream,
Until the final sound
And the final ray of light
Go out.
And there, in the grave of the third degree
Of nonexistence,
I meekly wait
To wake up cured
In the third dream,
In the second dream,
In the first dream…

Prayer

Source of all things,
Geometrical place in the void
That demands to be filled
To come into being;
Path by which you enter
A place where nothing exists
If it hasn't been pronounced;
Let the syllables
Fall
From your holy mouth,
And penetrate me
And plant the seed,
Make me put forth answer-plants
From which will grow out of
Silence supreme
Trees of sound
So the autumn winds can shake out meanings.

The Calendar

The calendar that I myself
Write on the wall
Is the only thing in the world
That I'm afraid of.
Every night my hand
Happily circles the number of the day:
Red for poetry
Green for prose
Or it trembles, fearful and ashamed
And marks down two crossed lines
Over the day expelled from time.
In this case,
My life is shortened
By the unknown lost in the void
That I haven't been able to write about,
Not a single letter that would anchor it in being.
My life is shortened
By every day that isn't protected by the red circle
Or the green circle,
Because whatever isn't written down
Doesn't exist.

Despot

I would like to live in his skull
Not just because
My mere presence there
Would constitute a guarantee
Of death,
But because this pilgrimage
To the scene of the events
Could help me to understand
Something,
Going mad myself,
Of course,
Squirming in beneath the cramped vaults
And through the narrow niches
Where logic never fit
And finally falling out
Like a sated worm
Fat with the forbidden fruit
That has tainted the universe.

Sieges

Besieged by life
And besieged by death,
We move inside a narrow space
Beyond whose walls
Our enemies wait
For our provisions to run out,
Provisions of bullets, of food, of fuel,
Of hope, of humour, of faith, of love.
When nothing is left at last,
Life and death will wait a while longer
And then they will enter the city arm in arm,
Amazed by those who put up such resistance,
And most of all by the reason why,
But neither of them has time to answer
Since they're both in a rush,
And they've already wasted a lot of time
And other sieges are waiting,
Others besieged
By life or by death.

The Same

Push out beyond
The borders of the darkness,
Enlarge by at least a fraction of an inch
The empty, luminous place
That blinds you and bars your
Sight, like darkness.
The fact is
All of it scares you to the same degree,
What you understand and
Also what you don't understand,
And what you can make out
In what you can't go into:
At every moment defeated the same,
Blinded the same with every evening sun.

Light and Words

Sea without fish,
Or algae,
Or seagulls,
So beautiful
Its beauty suffices to itself,
Enough to hide the mermaids
From a sun with the name of god
Who causes the light and the words
That he
Painfully
Extinguishes
Every night
In a pool of blood.

Sister

Sister of time
Who sends out armies into sleep
As in a battle over the rooftops
Of the world,
Your power
Is able to mix together
Sleep and dream
Beyond the law,
Subtracting one from the other
Or, even guiltier,
Adding one to the other
In a single sin,
And afterwards, they merge again
In death from where you watch us, among
Battalions of angels,
Sister moon.*

---

* An allusion to Saint Francis of Assisi's 'Canticle of Creatures' (1225): 'Be praised, my Lord, through Sister Moon and the stars; / In the heavens You have made them bright, precious and beautiful.' [Tr.]

Newspaper

If they were enemies in battle or a war,
But it's only a race to the top of the ladder –
They elbow their way, they share out the spoils
And they live like worms in a rotting cadaver.
And so the country continues to breathe
In spite of this cancer that eats it away.
Oh Lord, if you can, please set them free,
The honest ones at least, at least for a day!
Don't be afraid, there's only a few,
If you can't see fit to set them free
Then please pay attention when they speak:
They aren't scoundrels, it's just that they're weak,
Children dissolved into a grown-up crew,
A bevy of scurrying crabs in the sea…

Dependent

Dependent on the sun, the clouds, the shade,
Dependent on leaves and flowers and glades,
      on the shifting wind
      that always blows and trembles
In the trees, foreboding the rains
And the coming and going of the cranes.

Dependent on women and men,
On the thanks of the living, on the hoards of the dead,
On my own years, illumined, or stupid instead,
      but mostly, all used up.
O Lord, let me go, let me go,
From time and space, from ancestors and children,
From women and from men,
And from myself, if you can!

So I can laugh without the bitter falling of leaves,
So I can cry without the swelling of waves in the sea,
So I can leave without dragging the world in my wake
Like a tablecloth scattered with glasses and plates
      all broken and confused
And mixed with the wine and the food.

Let me be free, alone at last
And only guilty before my page.

That Day

Some say they'll come back
To look for their bodies,
Others see that day
Only as a great assembly
Of fine, transparent silhouettes
Cut out of
Their time-worn memories.
But strangely,
No one is afraid,
As though it were a party
Instead of a trial.
As though by then
All evil will have suddenly
Ended
Through the power of a single order
And everything were going to start anew
On its own
Like an undeserved
Reward,
Superstition
Or echo,
Of that disconcerting
Ray of light,
Incomprehensible.

To Get Out

Knock, knock, knock –
I say to the stone –
I want to get out,
I don't know who locked me up in here,
Who set me on this pedestal
Gripping my heels,
My hand lifted up, my eyes all white.
It hurts me, I say to the stone,
My arms have gone to sleep,
My legs are frozen stiff.
I want to get out,
Get down,
Forget –
About it all
Or only move on to another state of being.

Consequences

I long for those things
That I can't imagine,
Things that I know
Will only happen when I don't exist any more,
Mysterious beings
Who will follow me
And link me with miracles
That I can't even begin to suspect.
Descendants, as lost as I am in the world,
Connected to me,
Existing because I also once existed,
And I, in turn, tied
By a slender stem of blood
To who knows whom,
Crucified under an andesite sun
Two thousand years before.

> I long for them and they frighten me –
> All the things I've been and will be
> Without being asked.
> A hazy nostalgia
> For a future
> I'll be happy to escape from.

Hölderlin*

Waves of sunlight and water flow across the ceiling
And stain the scraps of paper
Covered with lines of scribbled verse
That madly gallop
Through infinite decades
Protected by the the carpenter and City Hall.

What more could a poet wish for
Than this round room where
The light turns into a river
And the river, light
And, lacking paper,
Its flowing covers everything just
As words, interwoven,
Overlap each other
On the backs of the steeds of madness
That gallop without halt
A decade, two, three, four
Through the waves of the ceiling?

What more could a poet wish for
Than the friendship of the carpenter
A decade, two, three, four,
Till no one knows
Which one is the poet and which one is the carpenter
When they go out together from the shimmering waters of the house
And ride into the darkness
On the backs of the dun-coloured steeds of madness...

---

* The German Romantic poet Friedrich Hölderlin (1770-1843) went mad
after the death of his beloved Susette Gontard. His upkeep for the last 36 years
of his life was paid for by the state and he was placed in the care of a carpenter,

Meanings

Meanings:
Boulders covered by a sea
Of many colours
By the hours of the day, the hours of centuries,
Fleeting
Unflinching meanings,
Half-buried in the sand,
The water smooths their lines,
Rounds them down,
Defeats them,
It gives them a constantly changing face,
And I see nothing more
Than the ebb and flow of a handful of meanings
Re-echoed in the falsifying wave
That is always so harsh
As it comes and goes
Over the sunken stones,
The ebb and flow of a handful of meanings
That hear
The questions, but not
The answerer nor the answer.

Ernst Zimmer, who had read *Hyperion* and who took him into his house in Tübingen. The room Hölderlin lived in was located in a tower of the old city wall that overlooked the river Neckar. Its large windows reflected the river's water onto the ceiling. Due to a shortage of paper, Hölderlin wrote his poems over previous ones. The poet and carpenter became so close that they both died in the same year. [Tr.]

Within a Pod

Because I haven't hulled myself
Into other similar beings
All ages are still enclosed in me
Like seeds asleep in a pod,
Too happy to try to break free of their coffin.
I examine myself in vain:
I see a single being
That hasn't changed for decades
In which I only know that
A girl, an adolescent, a woman
Are sleeping…
All hidden, one inside the other,
Refusing to bear fruit.

Our Century

Our century is the century gone by;
We've become our own history.
Strange, this sensation of a destiny concluded
While we still go on existing!
The raw material of those changes
That set the new millennium in motion,
Victims of earthquakes
Floods and revolutions
That are no longer meant for us,
We're faced with accomplished facts
Like a seed in the ground
About which all is known: what plant will bloom,
What fruit it will bear,
But not when it will decide
To die.

Degraded Sonnet

Temple ruins are the loveliest of temples
And dead gods most deserving of devotion,
Columns standing still, no breath, no motion,
Like amazing magnificent bones, the simple

Splendid skeleton of time, so much
Purer than when it lived, hidden in the skin,
The roar of dried-out seas and trumpets on the wind,
Echoes of surrounding battles long ago.

Everything is peaceful now. The gods have turned
Into poems. There is no time for the soul of the world
To take on a name, to take on a face.

Miracles have vanished. And even if one occurred,
There's no one in the desert now to witness it unfurl.
Faith, like stones ground down into sand, nearly erased.

Transvestite

Suddenly this transvestite
Behind which I've serenely
Spent the whole of a life
Cannot take off,
It's sprouting slender roots
Like the threads
That tie it to me,
A me that
I can't push away,
Memories lost in old-fashioned photos,
I no longer know what I wanted to hide,
I don't recall what I was like
But I'm amazed by what I am:
Skulls with cherries on their ears,
Children with greying hair,
Forgotten fruits
Withered
On the boughs.

God of Pastors

God of pastors and poets,
You build your oracles from the entrails of birds,
From the entrails of mountains,
You design incomprehensible
Solutions of words,
Redemptions that have to be deciphered first;
Compassionate force
That can kill the snake
But then feels guilty
After killing it,
Power that refuses to win,
Just as the light
To atone for its victory
Gives birth to a village of shadows.
O Lord! You carry the lamb
On your shoulders now,
But you're still the one who once came riding on dolphins,
The same one, word of words,
Who learns to know himself,
Brother of the defeated snake,
Who tells the future, in atonement, in its stead…

The Question

I wanted to be
Like those springs
That give their water freely,
The more you ask for the more they have;
And I thought that I was
Until the question appeared:
If that which surges forth
So limpid
And unstoppable
Is tears,
Then who is the eye
And, above all, what does it see?

Quadrant

First the numbers disappear,
Heavy and blind
The needles meanwhile feel
The quadrant,
Without being able to believe
That they have nothing left to point to,
Which doesn't mean at all
That time doesn't exist.
On the contrary,
The whirlpool of its passing has thrown off
The measurements,
The torrent cannot now be divided
Into seconds, minutes, hours, millennia,
While, in desperation, the needles
Row chaotically in the air
Not even able to point to
The end of the world.

It's Nighttime

It's nighttime when the bell towers burn
From so much ringing of the bells
And they flutter like gigantic flames when they die.
Glory, glory that ends in
A roaring howl, in sparks
And sunset,
Soft light glimmering
And turning into ash
Above the earth and in the sky.
It's the end-night
In which everything begins again:
Take me there
Now.

On a Cathedral Façade

So close during so many decades
That the limits have rotted away
And fallen,
And substances have begun
To melt, bit by bit,
To decompose,
To ferment all together
The same ideas,
Common diseases.
Amazed, I wonder why a fruit
Has grown by mistake
In another tree,
The thought that everything could have been
Different.
Two branches
Grown from the same trunk
On a cathedral façade,
A history sculpted in stone
That no one knows
How to tell.

Mandala

The intense image of a diamond helps me
To escape from a confused watchfulness
Into the sudden illumination of a dream,
Interior splendour,
The shape of light traced out
With light in light,
Till all you can see
Is a mysterious combustion
That signifies everything.
Just as the white light-beam of the diamond
Breaks down into splinters of colour,
Just as the snake, when it bites its tail,
Becomes a ring,
Deep within their endless roots
The peoples of the world all fall into the same delirium.

In Memoriam*

Eternity curled with the force
Of the snake that swallows its tail and feeds on itself
The endless river that pushes upstream to its source
To return in the opposite direction,
The rounded darkness beyond
The daily pathway of the sun
That sets, and rises out of death again.

We all go into the sod
Only to be reborn, from seed to god,
Let this be heard
O Lord of the holy castle of words,
Of the eternal return to the desert
That occurs forever and ever.

The eternal return of those vessels
That sail beneath the floods
That inundate empires and altars
Of so many peoples and different cultures
And gods both murdered and revived,
Unknown, but brothers that live
In this incommensurable neighbourhood.

---

* Elegy written for the Romanian poet Ștefan Agustin Doinaș (1922-2002). [Tr.]

This Poem

This poem only lasts as long
As it takes you to read it.
       The next time you do
It will change
Because you will also have changed.
And, of course, it will change even more
       When read by somebody else.

It only exists in this
Evanescent mood
It has gathered together from
       What it finds within you.

A disappearing song –
       Like a leaf of paper
       Turning slowly in a stream
       Floating from place to place–
Whoever put it there
Whatever they wrote – or not
Irrelevant.

THE TRANSLATORS

Paul Scott Derrick is a Senior Lecturer (retired) in American literature at the University of Valencia. His main field of interest encompasses Romanticism and American Transcendentalism and their influences on subsequent artistic and intellectual manifestations of the 20th and 21st centuries. His critical works include *Thinking for a Change: Gravity's Rainbow and Symptoms of the Paradigm Shift in Occidental Culture* (1994) and *We stand before the secret of the world: Traces along the Pathway of American Transcendentalism* (2003). He has edited and co-translated into Spanish a number of critical editions of works by Ralph Waldo Emerson, Emily Dickinson (Spanish and Catalan), Henry Adams and Sarah Orne Jewett. He is co-editor, with Viorica Patea, of *Modernism Revisited: Transgressing Boundaries and Strategies of Renewal in American Poetry* (Rodopi, 2007) and is, with Norman Jope and Catherine E. Byfield, co-editor of *The Salt Companion to Richard Berengarten* (Salt, 2011). With Miguel Teruel, he has published a translation of Richard Berengarten's *Black Light* into Spanish (*Luz Negra*, JPM Ediciones, 2012); and with Viorica Patea, translations into English of Ana Blandiana's *My Native Land A4* (Bloodaxe Books, 2014), and *The Sun of Hereafter • Ebb of the Senses* (Bloodaxe Books, 2017), a Poetry Book Society Recommended Translation. He is currently coordinating a series of critical studies and Spanish translations of Emily Dickinson's early fascicles.

Viorica Patea is Professor of American Literature at the University of Salamanca, where she teaches American and English literature. Her published books include *Entre el mito y la realidad: Aproximación a la obra poética de Sylvia Plath* (Ediciones Universidad de Salamanca 1989), a study on Whitman, *La apología de Whitman a favor de la épica de la modernidad* (Ediciones Universidad de León, 1999) and *T.S. Eliot's The Waste Land* (Cátedra: 2005). She has edited various collections of essays, such as *Critical Essays on the Myth of the American Adam* (Ediciones Universidad de Salamanca, 2001) and, together with Paul Scott Derrick, *Modernism Revisited: Transgressing Boundaries and Strategies of Renewal in American Poetry* (Rodopi 2007). Her most recent publication is a collection of essays, *Short Story Theories: A Twenty-First-Century Perspective* (Rodopi 2012), which received the Javier Coy Research Award for the best edited book (2013) from the Spanish Association of American Studies. Her research interests include comparative studies in witness literature of East European countries. In collaboration with Fernando Sánchez Miret, she has translated from Romanian into Spanish the annotated edition of *El diario de la felicidad* by Nicolae Steinhardt (Sígueme 2007) and *Proyectos de Pasado* and *Las Cuatro estaciones* by Ana Blandiana (Periférica 2008, 2011). She is also co-translator, with Paul Scott Derrick, of Ana Blandiana's *My Native Land A4* (Bloodaxe Books, 2014), and *The Sun of Hereafter • Ebb of the Senses* (Bloodaxe Books, 2017), a Poetry Book Society Recommended Translation.